AF441550

Relax

ON VALENTINE'S DAY

Copyright © 2019 by Ethereal Creativity

Cover Design by: Ethereal Creativity

ISBN: 9798609926265

All rights reserved. No part of this book may be reproduced without written permission of the publisher, except for the purpose of book reviews.

Disclaimer: This book
is not intended as a substitute for the
medical advice of physicians.

Research has consistently shown that most physical and mental health problems are due to high stress levels. Doctors and psychologists recommend practicing relaxing activities such as journaling, drawing, or painting to reduce stress. Drawing and coloring mandalas are considered forms of mindful meditation. They have a profound calming effect, allowing people to take their mind off of problems from their everyday life.

Relax on Valentine's day was created with the purpose of helping people set some time aside from their busy schedule to draw and color mandalas as a form of practicing self-care. The intention of this book is to help people relax so they can improve their physical and mental health, therefore improving their overall quality of life.

Best regards!
Ethereal Creativity

Create Your Own Mandala

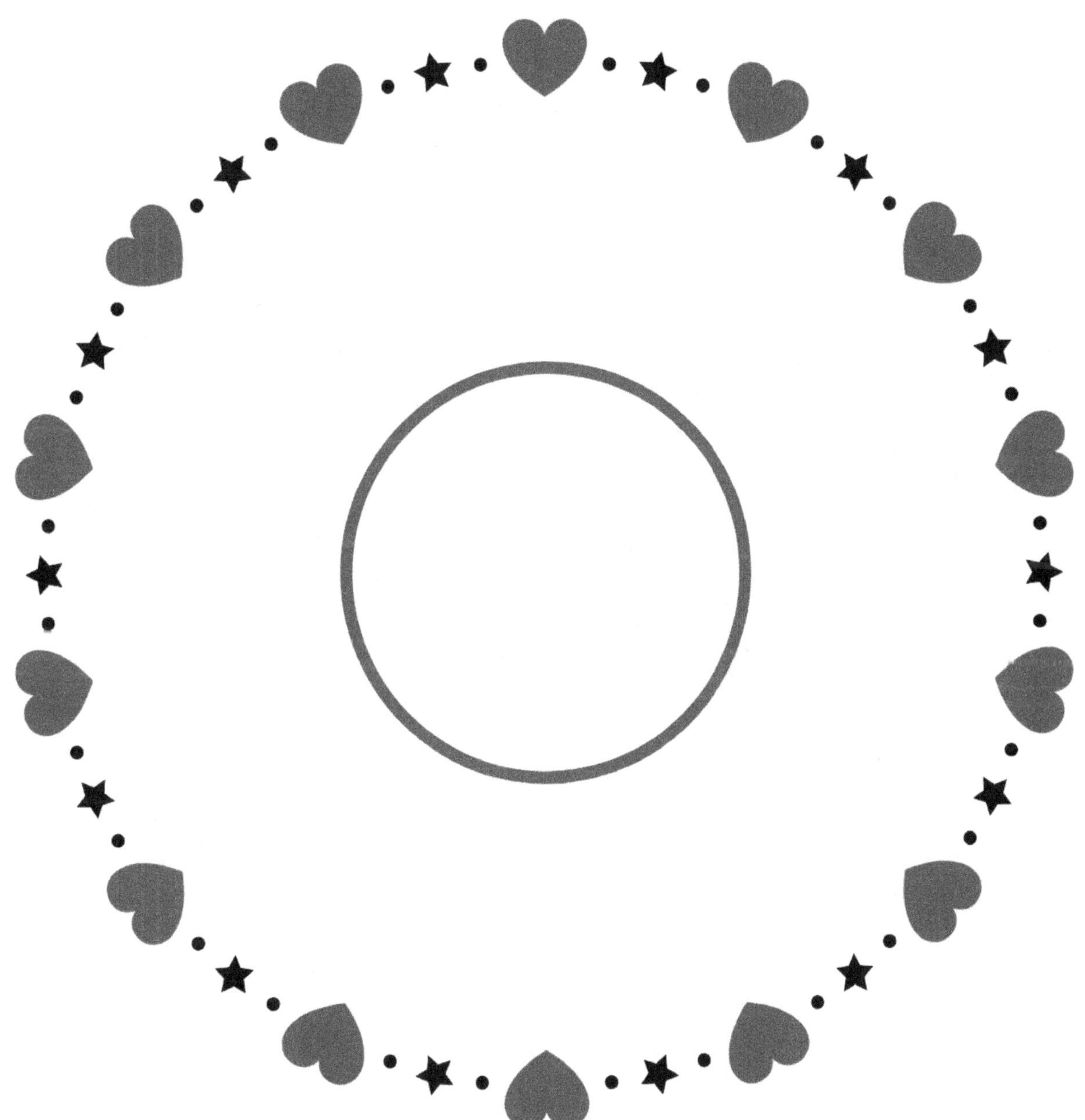

Create Your Own Mandala

Create Your Own Mandala

Create Your Own Mandala

Create Your Own Mandala

Create Your Own Mandala

Create Your Own Mandala

Create Your Own Mandala

Create Your Own Mandala

Create Your Own Mandala

Create Your Own Mandala

Create Your Own Mandala

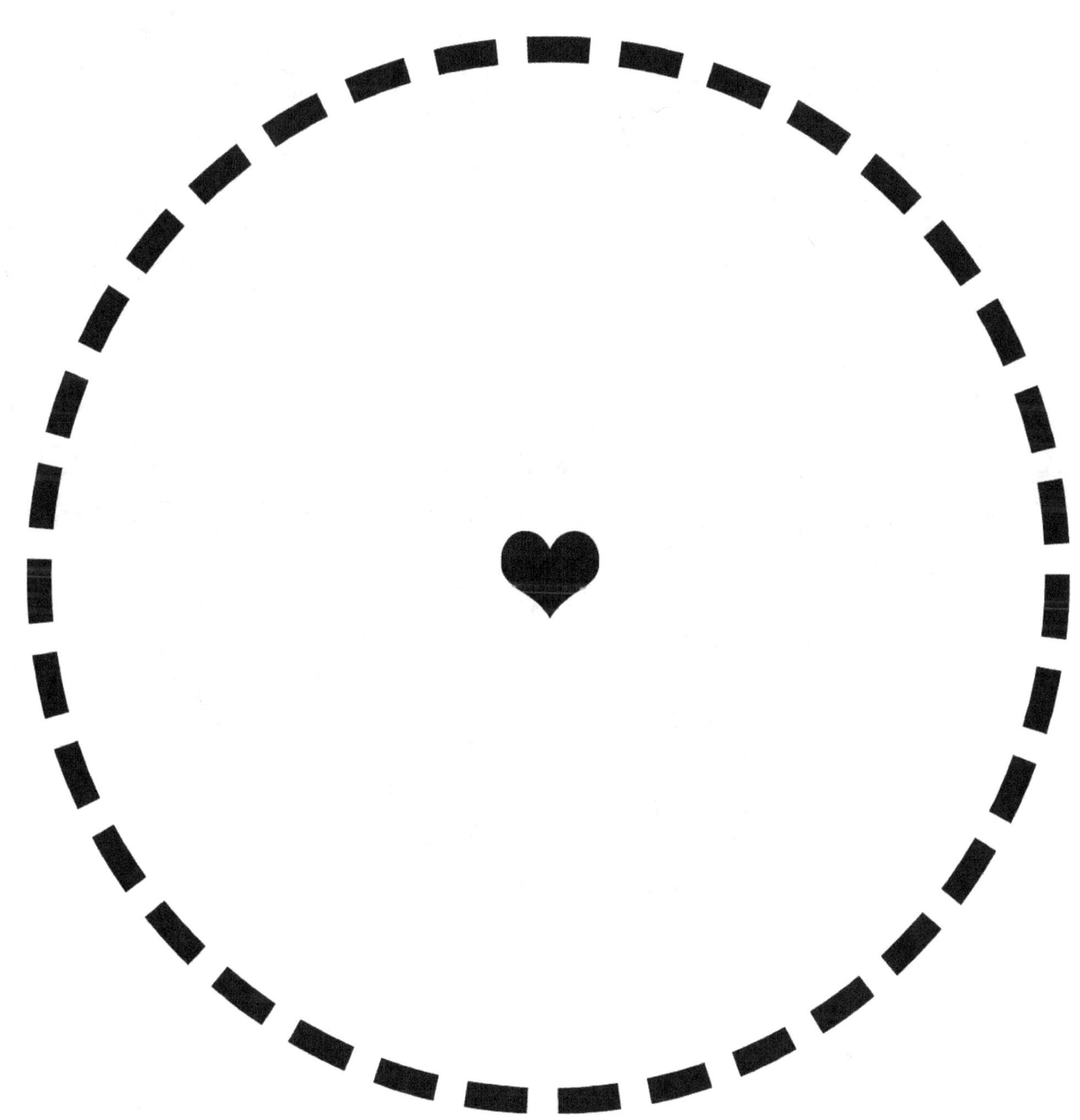

Create Your Own Mandala

Create Your Own Mandala

Create Your Own Mandala

Create Your Own Mandala

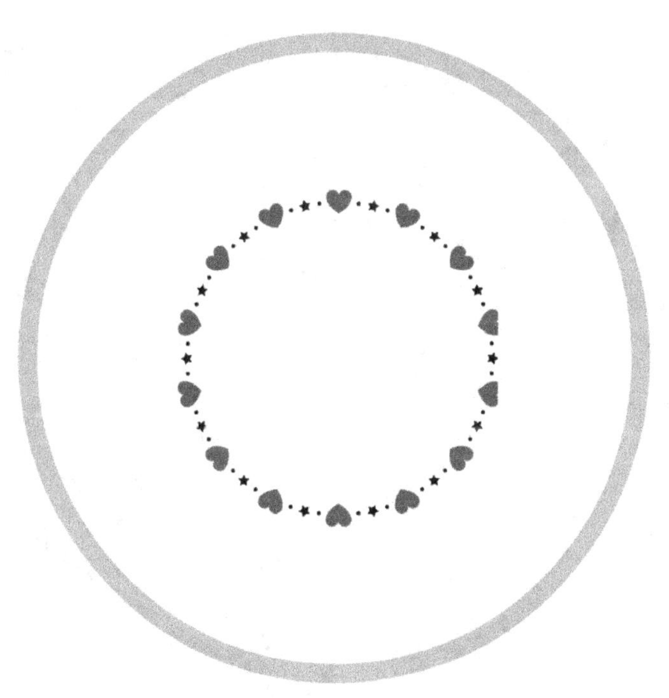

Create Your Own Mandala

Create Your Own Mandala

Create Your Own Mandala

Create Your Own Mandala

Create Your Own Mandala

Create Your Own Mandala

Create Your Own Mandala

Create Your Own Mandala

Create Your Own Mandala

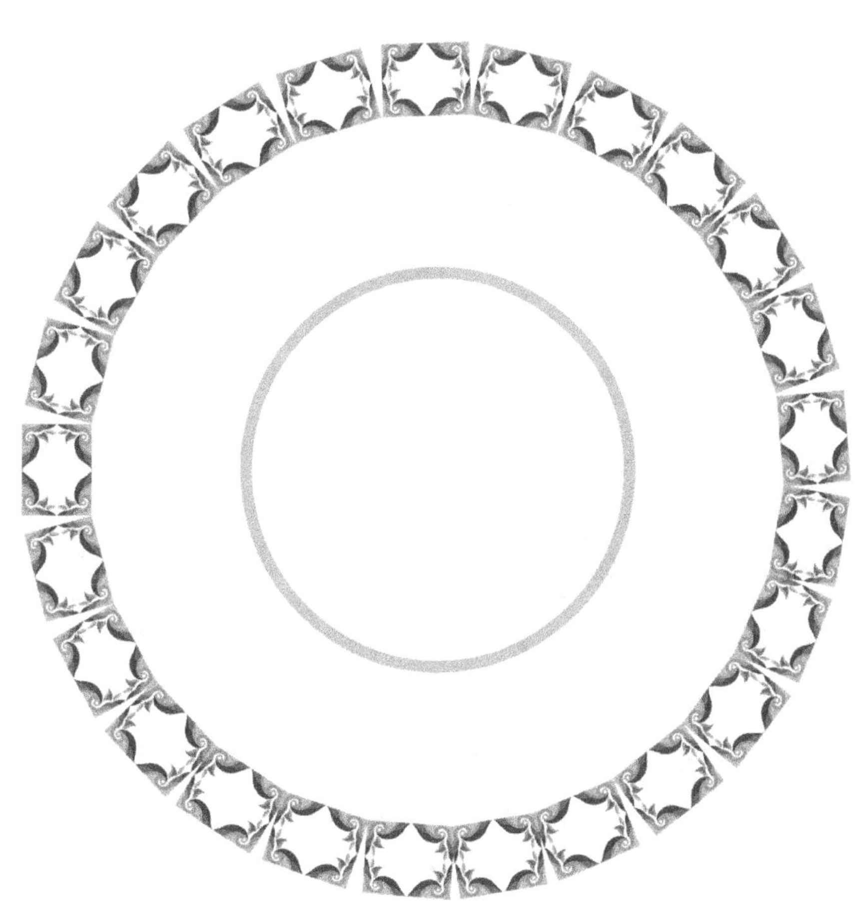

Create Your Own Mandala

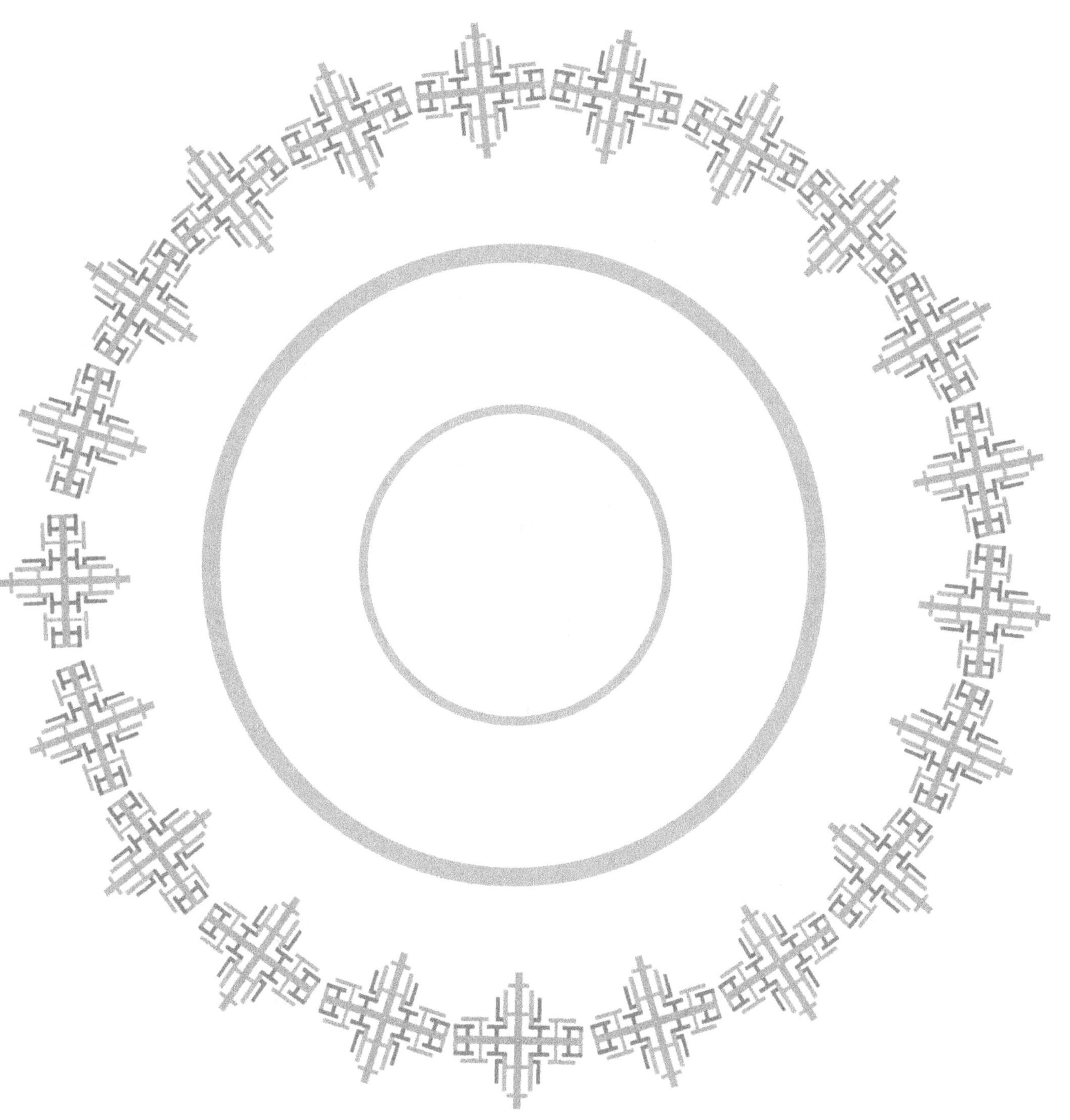

Create Your Own Mandala

Create Your Own Mandala

Create Your Own Mandala

BONUS

www.ingramcontent.com/pod-product-compliance
Lightning Source LLC
Chambersburg PA
CBHW060125120726
48003CB00009B/2783